Video Game Addiction Book For Families

15 Essential Things You Must Know About Video Game Addiction and Your Child.

Every year children spend over 90 billion dollars playing video games. 20% become addicted to the games and end up harming themselves and others around them.

In this revolutionary Itty Bitty® book, educator Sean Bryan shows you what to look for when evaluating the potential for addiction in your young Gamer. It shows how to recognize an addicted child and how to help your child break that addiction and return to living as a functioning member of your family and the community in which you live.

For example:

- Sudden development of academic decline
- Loss of social skills and Inability to communicate
- Loss of interest in members of the opposite sex
- Weight gain and loss of interest in physical activity.

Pick up a copy of this powerful book today and experience the joys and successes that come when your child is no longer addicted to Video Games.

Your Amazing Itty Bitty® Video Gaming Addiction Book

15 Essential Things You Must Know About Video Game Addiction and Your Child.

Sean Bryan

Published by Itty Bitty® Publishing
A subsidiary of S & P Productions, Inc.

Copyright © 2017 Sean Bryan

All rights reserved. No part of this book may be reproduced or transmitted in any form or by any means, electronic or mechanical, including photocopying, recording or by any information storage and retrieval system, without written permission of the publisher, except for inclusion of brief quotations in a review.

Printed in the United States of America

Itty Bitty® Publishing
311 Main Street, Suite D
El Segundo, CA 90245
(310) 640-8885

ISBN: 978-0-9992211-0-5

This book is dedicated to all the people who woke up from gaming and realized life had passed them by. Thank you Jon & Alison for helping me wake up!

Stop by our Itty Bitty® website to find interesting information regarding Video Game Addiction.

www.IttyBittyPublishing.com

or visit Sean at:

seanbryan32@yahoo.com

Table of Contents

Step 1.	Why is Video Gaming a Concern?
Step 2.	How Do I know if My Child is Addicted?
Step 3.	Are Educational Games Okay?
Step 4.	Should You Wean Your Child Off or Go Cold Turkey?
Step 5.	How Does Video Gaming Affect Your Child's Health?
Step 6.	Does Video Gaming Affect Your Child's Socialization?
Step 7.	Is Video Gaming Really Addictive?
Step 8.	What Should I **NOT** Do If I Think My Child's Addicted?
Step 9.	What Is The Worst Kind Of Video Game For Your Child? Why?
Step 10.	How Do You Get Control Back From The Game?
Step 11.	Are All video Games Bad?
Step 12.	Do Video Games Affect My Child's Performance At School?
Step 13.	I Play Video Games, Why Should I Be Concerned For My Child?
Step 14.	My Child Seems Fine Playing Video Games, Why Should I Be Concerned?
Step 15.	What Are The Enemies Of Healthy Gaming?

In this Itty Bitty Book you will find 15 simple things you can do to be aware of video game addiction in your children or spouse. You will find helpful facts, strategies, and advice to help you deal with this 21st century epidemic.

Step 1
Why Is Video Gaming A Concern?

More and more we see people disconnected from the reality around them. Often in coffee shops, friends sit together, looking at devices instead of communicating directly. As a teacher, I often have to deal with disruptive and defiant behavior – all due to video games.

1. 97% of youth play video games. That's over 64 million children. 80% of children can play without addiction. 1 in 5 are addicts - is that your child?
2. More kids ages 2-5 know how to play an app/game than know how to tie their own shoes.
3. Childhood obesity and other health concerns, such as eye strain, physical aggression and heart issues are on the rise, because kids aren't physically active. They sit in front of computer monitors, TVs, and phone screens.
4. Increased risk of ADD (Attention Deficit Disorder) or other learning disabilities are a result of video gaming.
5. Social issues are also on the rise. These issues include the inability to communicate, aggression, lack of socialization/appropriate behavior, or no interest in the opposite sex.

Have You Noticed?

The following are some common symptoms that people notice about their kids, and others. Most of these you will see in public, as well as private.

- Boys interested in games and not the girls sitting near them?
- One word or small phrase answers from your child? Most communication is an incomplete sentence or thought?
- Constantly on an electronic device?
- Increased aggression – both verbally and physically towards others?
- Tantrums if not given their own way?
- Poor hygiene?
- Poor appearance?
- No eye contact when speaking with or to people?
- No interests that are related to activities outside their devices, like hobbies, sports, or people?

Step 2
How Do You Know If Your Child Is Addicted To Video Games?

Addiction is addiction. Video game addiction or Internet Addiction, is relatively new, but nobody could predict what technology would do to us. Addiction is defined medically as:

1. The person needs more and more of the substance (game) to keep them going. (www.webmd.com)
2. If the person doesn't get more of the substance (game), they become irritable and miserable.
3. Psychology defines addiction as: an activity or substance, that can be pleasurable but with continued use becomes compulsive and interferes with ordinary life responsibilities.
4. Video Games increase Dopamine or the reward center in the brain.
5. Video Games fill several needs – A temporary escape. Games are social in a controlled way, they offer challenges with a purpose and instant reward/ gratification for success. and have constant measurable growth.

10 Possible Signs of Addiction
(from www.addictions.com)

- Mood shifts – extreme emotions
- Withdrawal – from conversations, leaving old friends, and not engaging even with you, the parent.
- Preoccupation – particularly with their game of choice.
- Poor Hygiene – lack of care about how they look and or smell.
- Physical Problems – eye strain, heart issues, increased weight gain, acne.
- Lack of School Performance – grades going down, or lack of care about grades at all.
- Loss of interest in other activities – such as sports or hobbies.
- Aggression – both verbal or physical.
- Isolation – spending more and more time away from everyone.
- Conflict with others – lack of skills to resolve problems in peaceful, socially acceptable ways.

Step 3
Are Educational Video Games Okay?

This is a question that I get asked often as an educator. The short answer is YES.

1. The newest information shows that educational games focus on one or two primary skills, and develop them.
2. The educational games do NOT activate the dopamine or "pleasure" center in the brain, but focuses on other specific parts.
3. Think of Educational Video Games as a more modern "Sesame Street" rather than an action movie.
4. The newest information about education video games says that the skills being developed are in a fun, interactive way.
5. Computers/technology will always be with us, and the focus of these education games is to grow.
6. Many of these games take the place of the drudgery of old fashioned flash cards.

What Skills Pay The Bills?

Here are a list of skills that Educational video games will focus on. You can read the back of the box, most games will list area(s) they are developing.

Educational games:

- Focus on manual dexterity.
- Develop reasoning abilities.
- Increase analytical skills.
- Focus on thinking in 3D.
- Using Spatial Navigation.
- Increase and use of memory.
- Basic grammar.
- Complex math – without physical flash cards, that always get misplaced or lost.

They may also help your child think fast – making quick decisions based on use of evidence.

Step 4
Should You Wean Your Child Off Of Video Games Or Go Cold Turkey?

This is a very difficult topic. The reason is how addicted is your child to video games? How do they react when their main outlet is taken away? What are you willing to do about it? How much can you handle? How much can they handle?

1. According to the experts, cold turkey is the hardest way to stop any addiction.
2. Cold Turkey requires your child to be aware of their addiction, admit to it, and want to change.
3. It also requires a lot of discipline!
4. What are you replacing with? Most Gamers withdraw to a fake world to avoid issues in the real world. Are you willing to face all these issues with your child?
5. In China there are camps to "rewire" video game addict's brains – they involve intense physical exertion and negative reinforcement around the devices.
6. Videos show children holding phones in their mouths as they are doing pushups!

Low and Slow, Wins All the Time!

Weaning off is the preferred and more successful way according to the experts.

- Start by tracking time of game play, and problems/behaviors that have developed from this addiction.
- If you wish to try it alone, you can start by setting limits to how long your child can play and slowly reduce it over time.
- Psychologist highly suggest therapy for this – individual, family, or group therapy.
- Therapy is good because it helps with the underlying issues – emotional or social or both.
- There are camps for Video Game addiction, and your child may need a change of behavior/habits.
- Best thing –

YOU DON'T HAVE TO DO IT ALONE!

Step 5
How Does Video Gaming Affect Your Child's Health?

Video games hit the pleasure centers in your brain. This pleasure comes at a cost. As a child becomes more and more involved in gaming, they will push themselves physically to be the best. The short term gains have long term consequences. As a teacher I see many issues that students have.

1. Students that are addicted physically twitch in their seats and cannot sit still for long.
2. Many of these children can't read for extended periods of time, their attention span is too short.
3. Physically, we are seeing as a nation, an extreme amount of obesity in children.
4. Many of these students are obsessed with caffeine/energy drinks, and all the negative attributes associated with ingesting large amounts of it.
5. Children often fall asleep in class because they were up all night gaming.
6. If a child is corrected, they become aggressive. This aggression is displayed physically and verbally.

What do the doctor's see?

Both psychologists and family health care providers have listed the following as symptoms of addicted gamers:

- Neck Strain
- Eye strain & eye injuries
- ADD/ADDA issues. (Your child may be conditioned by the games to display similar movements and issues and be mislabeled/diagnosed with these issues.)
- Breathing issues, brought on by poor health, hygiene and obesity.
- Over weight
- Under muscular
- A fixation with caffeine
- Lack of sleep

Step 6
Does Video Gaming Affect Your Child's Socialization?

Y E S ! This is the biggest area of concern adults are facing with their children and video game addiction.

1. When an addict feels bad, he takes a hit of cocaine. When a gamer feels bad, he turns to his game and "plays".
2. Gamer addicts usually have social issues. They hide where they are emotionally "safe" in a comfortable digital world.
3. That means we have 21-year-olds who are emotionally 12, and don't know how to handle an adult world.
4. People online can say and do virtually anything without too many concerns or consequences. Because games let your child create a character name, he or she is anonymous.
5. Anonymity + audience with no social pressures = negative behaviors like: Sexual harassment, bigotry, racism, foul language. With this secret identity, do you know if your child is a superhero or a supervillain?

Questions To Ask Yourself

- What are the social norms in games?
- Is your child learning how to interact appropriately with people of the same sex?
- Is your child learning how to interact with people of the opposite sex in a manner you approve of?
- Can your child work properly in a group?
- Is your child able to verbalize/ communicate properly? Complete thoughts and sentences when he or she speaks? Use socially acceptable language?
- Do you want your son or daughter to learn how to be a man or woman from a game? What kind of person will they be? What are they experiencing?
- Can they act in a fitting manner when corrected, challenged, or working with others?
- If your child is showing signs of arrested development, how long do you want to live with a child at that emotional level?

Step 7
Is Video Gaming Really Addictive?

This is a highly controversial topic. Because technology and its growth is so rapid, it is hard for scientist to see the long-term effects of Gaming. As a first generation gamer, I say it is addictive, because of what it has done to me and others like me who are/were gamers. Keep in mind:

1. By spending time on a game, that is time gone that cannot be recovered. We are social creatures, and the limited time on this planet can be used to learn, help and interact with others.
2. Now we have put a physical device, an in-between interface, between people and their interactions.
3. Video games are an escape from reality, but more and more time is being spent in games. That's the prime definition of addiction.

Interactions, You Be The Judge!

Here are some behaviors that can indicate addiction

- Does your child sit in the corner crying and not eating because he or she had a game taken away/didn't get their way?
- Has your child become violent?
- Is he/she quick to anger or rage at an inappropriate level for the situation?
- Does your child appear depressed? For example: wearing black cloths, makeup, depressing music or a lack of engagement with the people around.
- Has your child slowly given up on a sport or hobby? Loss of interest in anything that isn't related to the game?
- What is the game replacing? Is your child riding their bike, hanging out with friends, fixing a toy, playing a sport?
- One of the truest ways to get a reaction is to take away the game for a small period of time. How does your child handle it?
- What are the games teaching your child? Shooting is okay? Hurt others before talking? Never listen or respect others?

Step 8
What You Should *Not* Do If You Suspect Your Child Is Addicted To Video Gaming?

Do you think that your child may be addicted to games? If you do it is time to find out if they are and to get the appropriate help.

1. Don't force them to go cold turkey! If your child isn't ready to quit their addiction, going cold turkey will have unpredictable results. Meaning, they can become violent. There are many YouTube videos showing their reactions.
2. Cold turkey requires your child to want to step away from their games first. (Remember, their game has been their comfort bubble to protect them from the big, mean, unfair world.)
3. It requires a lot of self-discipline to say "no" when they've always said "yes".
4. This is harder today, with digital games on portable devices that can be played whenever and wherever they are.
5. This is a very confrontational approach. Do you want an argument or fight? Will they be reasonable and follow through? Statistically, no. This just leads to more problems, and the child will feel they can't talk to you if/when they are ready.

You think You Are Extreme?

This internet gaming addiction is a worldwide problem. Many different people have different ways to deal with it.

- Problem: In China, people have died in internet cafes playing marathon-long video games!
- Solution: China has created a boot camp for addicts. The children dress in military clothing and complete in a great deal of hard physical labor.
- Problem: Teen girl always on phone, talking back to dad, and not doing her choirs.
- Solution: A famous YouTube video has a Montana rancher shooting his daughter's phone as punishment for the problem. The child cries and describes how she feels cut off from the world.
- Problem: Adult son lives at home, with no job, playing games and doesn't go to school.
- Solution: Father takes all the system and games outside and sits atop a riding lawn mower. Son refuses to look for work – dad destroys the games and system.

Step 9
What Is The Worst Kind of Video Game For My Kids? Why?

As a recovering semi-pro gamer, I get asked this all the time. After researching it, even I was surprised by the answer. First, we need to know what types of games are out there.

1. Action games: Platform games, shooter games (Black Ops), fighting games(Street Fighter).
2. Action-Adventure: Stealth (Thief), Survivor Horror, & Metroidvania (Metroid, Castlevania side scrollers).
3. Adventure Games: Text (MUDs), graphic (Discworld), Visual novels, etc…
4. Roll-Playing: Action(Diablo), MMORPG (World of Warcraft).
5. Simulation: Life (SIMS), Vehicle (Flight simulators), Construction/Management (Railroad Tycoon).
6. Strategy: 4x(Civilization), Artillery (Scorched), RTS(Starcraft), MMORTS, Real Time tactics (RISK), Tower Defense (Clash of Clans)
7. Sports: FIFA,

Take a Ride into the Danger Zone.

The worst one is MMORPGs! (Massive Multiplayer Online Roll Playing Games like World of Warcraft or Grand Theft Auto.) Here's why these are the worst:
- They are the most "social" games and offers temporary escape with people just like your child.
- Persistent world that always is on and your character always can gain/grow, so you always want to do more and stay on longer.
- Clans/Guilds/groups that are easy to team up with and play and achieve goals.
- In-game chat, use of headsets to talk to, customizable characters to look like anything you want.
- People with similar likes. Interests, beliefs, values, & social issues.
- Challenges have a purpose and success is clear, not so much in real life.
- Constant measurable growth. You can visit websites to cheat and get ahead, not so much in real life.
- Constant flood of virtual achievements, heroic deeds.
- Arrogant behavior because they've mastered an area in a game, and think it applies to real life when it doesn't.
- All-in-all they create an illusion and make it difficult to break away from it because of all of its reinforcements.

Step 10
I Feel So Helpless, How Do I Get Control Back From the Video Games?

Remember why you are doing this, it's about your children and the life you want them to achieve. They cannot do that in a virtual world, they have to build their lives in the real world. They have to learn to face their fears, rejections, awkwardness, and see that they are unique, special individuals. It's that specialness that many children are missing from their lives.

1. You control everything financially, and that means there are passwords and settings for everything. Use the tools you are provided with.
2. Show your child that real life is more exciting than the virtual, fake one. Life is to be experienced. We weren't made to sit in front of a computer screen for hours at a time.
3. Remember the phrase, "It takes a village to raise a child". Don't do it alone. There is always help out there. Ask for help from your family and friends. This doesn't make you a bad parent. <u>You are doing something, & that is good parenting!</u>
4. Get professional assistance.

Tools For Your Toolbox!

- Log when and how long your child plays. No one can argue with facts!
- Log problems you've seen resulting from gaming. Behavior, grades, social interactions, hygiene.
- How does your child react to time limits?
- Many games and controls have parental settings and places to enter passwords. Use them all! There are free apps that are password generators that create what you need.
- Password your: internet connection, wifi connection, phones, & computer/platforms. With passwords, don't make it easy like your first name backwards. Use a random key generator. You can always write down the password or put it in your notes on your phone, so your child can't use it.
- There are camps for gamers.
- Talk to a therapist or psychologist, use your village.
- Make goals. Do "X" chores, you get "Y" time on the game.

Step 11
Are All Video Games Bad?

This is a controversial topic. A 2013 study says no. If we look at the numbers, they show a different story. 20% of all children who play are addicted. That is too high to be accepted. What happens to a society when that many people are addicted to the same thing, it crumbles.

1. First Person Shooters train children to shoot, move quickly, react, and not think about consequences. They are able to respawn, so dying is okay, not truly dead. That's not how real life works.
2. Ever seen a female character in a game? Hypersexualization of their body parts. No wonder boys aren't talking to girls; they don't look like what they see on the screen.
3. Last year the video game industry made over 99 Billion dollars! Are you sure they have your child's best interests at heart or are they just in it for a profit?
4. Strategy & tactic games have a small amount of merit, but they activate the wrong parts of our brains.
5. Educational games are very intentional and are safe, in small amounts.

Bad to the Bone

- January 2016, saw the release of the first commercial virtual reality goggles. If we have 20% addicted, and now they will be fully immersed visually and auditorily, what do you think will happen? This device is a direction connection to the pleasure center of our brains. Scary!
- The brain isn't able to tell the difference between real life and virtual with these goggles. We will have PTSD in gamers. The military already have issues with drone pilots and VR helmets. Now we are doing this to our children?!
- Video Game addiction isn't recognized by health care providers because they don't have enough people nor training to handle the epidemic. Who will help your child?

Step 12
Do Video Games Affect My Child's Performance at School?

Many teachers I work with can tell if a student is a gamer or not. They know because of the student's social behaviors as well as academic issues.

1. Academically, most gamers are only gaining surface information. They are able to find information quickly, but aren't able to use it or connect it with other areas.
2. Gaming students look for a quick answer and cannot explain, rationalize, or use information & make deeper connections. They are looking for key words, not key ideas.
3. Gamers have ADD/ADHD characteristics. They have difficulty reading long passages, so they miss answers to questions.
4. Gamers tend to not raise hand and blurt out the answers. They don't give any others a chance to answer or win or be right.
5. Students who game tend to act without thinking or consideration, they are reactive. This is an issue in groups.

I Spy With My Good Eye, My Child's School Work Habits.

- Does your child always say they have "nothing" for homework and just play games? Every high school and most middle school subjects have homework.
- Does your child look at or even show you their agendas?
- How are their backpack and folders arranged? Are things in a logical, easy to find manner?
- Does your child come straight home and just plop on the couch and play games?
- Is your child doing their chores or homework right away when they get home?
- How are their grades? Are they dropping, even though your child is always online?
- Is your child lying to you? Do you even know? If they are evasive, they are trying to hide something. They may even be hiding it from themselves.

Step 13
I Play Video Games, Why Should I Be Concerned? This is Family Time.

This is a common question or statement I get from gamers. They are older and have kids, and wonder all the time why this is an issue. They are obviously in that 80% of not being addicted. Let's look at it more closely.

1. Your brain as an adult is fully protected. It's done developing and modifying. Most the current neural patterns have harden and the most used ones are quicker than the less used ones.
2. Think about a child's brain. It is still developing. Would you just put a baby in front of a TV with all its flashing images and sounds?
3. You are doing just that with your child's brain. It doesn't have the cognitive ability to defend itself nor the ability to filter between good and bad that quickly. (That's why we teach children all the time.)
4. These images flashing at the child will make it harder for the brain to learn. It will then develop or mimic ADD/ADHD behaviors, along with other health concerns.

Move Over Beaver, it's Father & Son Time!

- What are you teaching your child when you play? To be a good leader, good sportsmanship, good teamwork? Not what I've seen.
- Most adults use headsets and are cursing at the game or other people playing a game.
- You're showing them it's okay to kill.
- Are you drinking when you are playing? How connected are you to your surroundings when you play?
- What I've observed are people playing the game trying to achieve a digital goal and ignoring real world achievements.
- How are you interacting with the rest of the family during game time?
- Are you showing your child that there is a difference between adult ways vs. a child's ways? Is it okay for them to do the same as you?
- Are you teaching leadership skills, organization, helping others, achieving goals?

Step 14
My Child Seems Fine Playing Video Games, Why Should I Be Concerned?

Congratulations, your child isn't an addict! There are still issues with online gaming that you should be aware of. The more sophisticated technology becomes, the easier it is for someone to use it as a tool against your child.

1. Who is your child playing with? Characters on the screen can be customized and look like anything or anyone. Are they playing with predators, adults, children their age, people with your same moral background, scammers? Are these people you would allow into your own home?
2. What are they playing? What kind of games is your child involved with? Are they team games? Is he a trained killer shooting people indiscriminately? Is he building something or taking things apart?
3. What is your child learning? Is he getting skills that pay the bills? Simulation piloting games? Is he/she learning how to ignore life/reality? How is this helping them when they face true adversity? Games have restarts, life does not.

You Got the Power!

- Parents control everything from buying the game, to having the ability to play the game.
- You buy the platform, controls, & games.
- You pay for the electricity to run the games.
- You pay the phone bill and for the internet.
- You control the Wi-Fi, any networks, modems, hubs, or LANs connections.
- Each one of these connections has to be okayed, authenticated, and approved. All of these are able to be given passwords. Each is a barrier for your child to get access to their addiction of choice.
- Since you pay for everything, the biggest issue I see: Never ever let you your child have access to your credit card/account information! This includes email accounts.
- It's too easy for scammers, hackers, to use your child to get your information and take advantage of you.
- Don't let your child make a "friend" in-game without you knowing about it. There are stories of children running away to their in-game friend.

Step 15
What Are the Enemies Of Healthy Gaming?

There are many ways that gaming can be fun and rewarding. Steps have to be taken, and you must be aware of all the dangers online. You are letting your child experience them all online unprotected, if you don't monitor or set up protections.

1. Biggest issue is justification of actions. "One more minute/ adventure/ round/ achievement". This is a dangerous slide towards addiction.
2. It's only entertainment. Games are fun and relaxing, there's nothing wrong with shooting animations.
3. This is family time. We can all play the same game. There is no difference between adults and children. This creates an unhealthy lack of roles.
4. I trust my child to do what's right. How does your child know if you've not taught them what is appropriate online behavior? If you scream at the screen, they will see that is okay and do the same.
5. What are they truly doing in the game? Are they creating or destroying?

Bad Elements:

- Peer Pressure, to get the newest game, spend more real money on fake things.
- Not setting parameters/limits. Children need boundaries and if not given any online, they will do great harm to themselves and others.
- They can play with anyone, people you don't know, and may not approve of.
- Playing anytime they want. Children need real world experiences and lots of sleep for healthy growth.
- Trying to play at a competitive level. This takes lots of time, skill, money, dedication, research, and sometimes teamwork. Is a game really worth all this energy? What are they getting out of it?
- Needing or wanting more and more playing time.
- Socialization skills in real world stagnated, and socializing with the wrong elements online.
- Parent controls turned off!

You've finished. Before you go...

Tweet/share that you finished this book.

Please star rate this book on Amazon.

Reviews are solid gold to writers. Please take a few minutes to give us some itty bitty feedback on this book.

ABOUT THE AUTHOR

Sean Bryan has been video gaming since the industry was born. He's played on every system until 2010. Sean was a semi-pro video gamer who trained two players that became professional players. His addiction of choice was World of Warcraft.

Sean Bryan has been teaching for fifteen years. He is actively involved in his school, running two clubs during lunchtime. Sean loves teaching English, and History. He sneaks into the Science classes to hear all the new information, particularly about Space.

Sean Bryan quit gaming cold turkey, with the help of his mentors Jon & Alison. Sean spends most of his time with his friends and family.

He can be reached at: seanbryan32@yahoo.com

If you like this Itty Bitty® book you might
Also enjoy these best selling books…

- Your Amazing Itty Bitty® **Communicating With Your Teenager Book** – Christine Alisa, MS

- **Your Amazing Itty Bitty® Family Leadership Book** – Jacqueline T. D. Huynh

- **Your Amazing Itty Bitty® Parenting Teens Book** – Gretchen E. Downey

Or the many other Itty Bitty® Books available on line.

www.ingramcontent.com/pod-product-compliance
Lightning Source LLC
Chambersburg PA
CBHW061305040426
42444CB00010B/2522